HONEST ENGINE

OTHER TITLES BY KYLE DARGAN

The Listening (University of Georgia Press, 2004)

Bouquet of Hungers (University of Georgia Press, 2007)

Logorrhea Dementia (University of Georgia Press, 2010)

HONEST ENGINE

poems

KYLE DARGAN

The University of Georgia Press *Athens & London*

© 2015 by the University of Georgia Press
Athens, Georgia 30602
www.ugapress.org
All rights reserved
Designed by Erin Kirk New
Set in Garamond Premier Pro and Le Havre
Printed and bound by Sheridan Books
The paper in this book meets the guidelines for
permanence and durability of the Committee on
Production Guidelines for Book Longevity of the
Council on Library Resources.

Most University of Georgia Press titles are
available from popular e-book vendors.

Printed in the United States of America
19 18 17 16 15 P 5 4 3 2 1

Library of Congress Cataloging-in-Publication Data

Dargan, Kyle.
  [Poems. Selections]
  Honest engine : poems / Kyle Dargan.
    pages cm
  Includes bibliographical references.
  ISBN 978-0-8203-4728-8 (pbk. : alk. paper) —
  ISBN 0-8203-4728-0 (pbk. : alk. paper)
  I. Title.
  PS3604.A74A2   2015
  811'.6—dc23

                        2014011857

British Library Cataloging-in-Publication Data available

Sooner or later, it all comes crashing down (crashing down),

crashing down (crashing down) when everyone's around.

~N.E.R.D.

SCHEMATIC

WITHIN THE BREAK: AN AUTHOR'S NOTE

This is the sound of blues breaking
the broken back together

~FRED JOINER

My previous book, *Logorrhea Dementia*, ended with the Rapture. This collection begins at a rupturing.

By age thirty-one, I had never been punched in the face, and I had never broken a bone in my body—this despite being born in an angry city and spending ages eleven through seventeen roving the testosterone-rich halls of an all-boys' school. While I had lived far from an unchallenging life, I had yet to learn certain things about hurt—significant items were missing from my pain résumé.

The year prior, my grandmother, Ruth Dargan—who was a constant and influential presence during my childhood—ended her brief battle with cancer. In the best sense, she had lived a long and exhausting life. With all she made from the breaths she took, there was no reason to mourn the breaths she would never draw. I had accepted all that before I walked into her apartment with my father to see her for a final time—seeing being all that was possible given that she was in a medically induced coma. My father told me she could not hear me—though I did not need to be told. We touched her hands, told her we loved her, and then I walked out of the room while my father remained to tend to her linens. I took three steps before I fell against the hall's wall—having gone from resisting crying to being wracked with tears and retching. It was a pain that my body could not contain, likely because it was not sourced from within my flesh. It was the pain of one pillar of my world crumbling and burying me beneath debris. I would eventually dig myself free and find an altered landscape awaiting me.

The year following my thirty-first concluded with a succession of losses. First, my aunt, Marie Dargan, suffered, and died from, consecutive heart attacks. Next, my dear friend Marlene Hawthrone suffered a heart attack in Atlanta, though she was only twenty-nine and beginning to blossom. Lastly, and within a week of each other, my college roommate Bryan Rubin was hit

and killed by a car fleeing the Newark police and my stepfather's mother—
my last surviving grandmother, Remonia Williams—expired in East Orange
General Hospital.

Amid that flurry of sadness, though my face and body remained
unscathed, I began to realize that those deaths were my blows, my thresholds
of pain. The bloodied noses and broken collarbones I had yet to receive were
befalling me in the guise of losses. At times, I found myself punch-drunk but
also reshaped. It was not quite a transformative bout with, say, *duende*—for I
was not calling with abandon for death to come forward and wound me, and
even if I were, that would have been a battle with the external, as opposed
to *duende*'s cathartic darkness that one calls forth from within the self.
Nonetheless, that "beating" had rendered me common. The sadness of the
living—which bombards us from birth—had finally breeched and flooded
me, marked me same among men and women. But in becoming a survivor,
I found myself traversing a territory of time and space in which each day
I would find myself encountering some wrinkle of life, what I know of it,
without these figures walking beside me—an absence of their shadows.

With this personal epoch—when so many of those whose presence
buffered, if not disguised, the stark realities of my life are now gone—I
am seeing our human dilemma anew and questioning what can I afford to
continue believing. With maturation, there is mounting darkness, but I
cannot allow it to be all I see.

ACKNOWLEDGMENTS

Versions of these poems first appeared in the following venues:

Baffler: "The Robots Are Coming"
Connotation Press: "Dear Religion"
Copper Nickel: "States May Sing Their Songs of Praise"
Poets.org (Academy of American Poets): "A House Divided"
Rattling Wall: "Note Blue or Poem for Eighties Babies"
Subtropics: "Reverence in the Atomic Age"

"Note Blue or Poem for Eighties Babies" was also featured online as part of the "Arts and Academe" series from the *Chronicle of Higher Education* and anthologized in *The Hide-and-Seek Muse: Annotations of Contemporary Poetry.*

"The Robots are Coming" was also anthologized in *The Best American Nonrequired Reading 2014.*

"State of the Union" was included in the anthology *District Lines*, vol. II.

I would like to thank the following individuals for their support of this book: Sydney Dupre and Beth Snead for adopting and championing the project; Erika Stevens for her sharp eye and publishing guidance; Sandra Beasley for being willing to trade manuscripts as our books came together; Paulette Beete, Hayes Davis, and Melanie Henderson for sharing poems on Sunday mornings on Capitol Hill.

I would also like to thank the University of Iowa's International Writing Program, the Chinese Writers Association, and the U.S. Department of State for their support of the Life of Discovery program that allowed me to travel to China and engage with some of that nation's literary artists—which inspired a number of the poems in this collection.

EQUITY

STATE OF THE UNION

I live in a land called East of the River,
five miles from the U.S. Capitol,

where air space must still be policed—
no-fly zone. Tonight, a helicopter freezes
into a shallow star blinking above my house

while the men and women of government
herd themselves inside the Senate chambers—

our Commander in Chief and all his cabinet
save one, traditionally one, who is excluded
and tasked with waiting to resurrect

our country should Iran, Russia, China, or
what's left of Iraq try to bowl a ballistic seven-ten

split, toppling the Monument and Capitol.
Tonight, it's the agriculture secretary's duty
to save us. It should always be our agriculture

secretary. In times of crisis, a country needs—
before commerce or war or law—to eat,

and if Congress allowed the appointment
of an agriculture secretary who can't grow
a pea, might we not deserve oblivion?

I prefer to imagine our Secretary of Agriculture
hunkered in his undisclosed location,

listening to the speech on battery-powered radio,
sifting seed through his dusty palms, deciding
what must grow first in the aftermath of fire.

OWNERSHIP

I wrap *home* in quotation marks
when writing of my mother's
hulking house in New Jersey
ever since I signed my name
to a mortgage for my dwelling
two-hundred miles south of her.
I keep the key to my mother's doors
on the ring with my office key—
my two "homes" away from this
new house. I live in D.C.
Once, I told my family, *No one lives
in D.C.—Virginia and Maryland, elsewhere.*
Now my territory is the taxpayer's turf.
My homeland will ever be my mother's
sallow Victorian—I belong to that house
more than it belongs to me, that house
a "home" only when I choose to visit her,
see her. Who sees D.C.? No one—
so, now I am a no-one living inside
a brick façade. I tell Aunt Marie
I'm heading home. *New Jersey,* she asks.
No, *home* not "home." I could say
house, but back "home" to house
means to dominate. Wells Fargo
actually owns me, my house.
D.C. claims jurisdiction over the dirt
where my house rests its bones.
My mother still owns our "home,"
while I write checks and post them
to the bank each month. They send back
small pieces of my house, which I sow
in this earth that bears none of our initials,

CHINA SYNDROME
or SLOW RIDE FROM LOGAN TO THE HEIGHTS

~for Elahe

In China, the transit coaches ride
on four legs with wheels for feet,
straddling any cars gridlocked below.
That is how my weary mind
wants to regale you once it's evident
we could have hoofed these ten blocks
faster than traffic will permit this 54 bus
we squeezed within—finding a seat beside
a Caucasian girl lecturing an Egyptian man
about Christopher Columbus. (*I mean*
who does that—comes to a country and says
I own you now? You know?)

In this moment—a blank-faced Salvadoran
giving us both the *you-hearing-this-shit* eye—
I realize why, of all the odd beauty I saw
in China, I mainly remember those buses.
Mere awe: not of the elevated carriages,
but of the fact that China grew tired of traffic
and resolved to venture a solution.

I am no communist [repeat], but I am tired
of waking vexed in this land of Cialis and picture-
in-picture-in-picture flat screens. I want
our American generation to cure something
major—erase one smudge from humanity's
horizon. When did it come to be
that good ideas only migrate here?
We used to yank them from our soil.

No one is looking at us.

Off the bus, you say that traffic is no major ill,
but you have never traveled to Beijing—
you have not seen its sky smogged through
to an opaque sadness. For you, I would
describe it, but for now, for argument's sake,
I need you to think of China as that broad,
beautiful place our promise abandoned us for.

O, GHOST

O, Ghost, you methane mirage, blue
burning at the foot of my basement stairs
ignited nightly by the haunting's hunt.
I have read you come hungry—a gullet
straw-thin, belly like a cavern, you vase
with limbs. I place cut asters down your throat.
They fall through you, to the floor. I pour
rainwater down your throat. It rises.
You want a Michelob. You want a good fuck
or some crystalline spark injected through
your phantom veins, but, Ghost, I am
the wrong dealer for you. I've read
parables suggesting *truth* is all you'll digest
at this point. I am only a heartbeat,
a sentient sack of blood who expects
night will give way to sunlight
as it has done each day of my life.
I cannot call that *truth*. Ghost, I cannot
feed you, but I'll tongue a woman wildly
for you. I'll feed pints of ale across my lips.
I'll rub my nerves raw with recklessness,
reminded now that this is all we ever were:
wrecks. Pity all who think they are heavenly
bodies marooned here on earth. We smolder.
We expire in trills of smoke. Ghost,
what arrogance earned you your body
of cold, ceaseless flame? Were my touch
so true, I would extinguish you.

I imagine each enunciation, each syllable
pronounced—*Mississippi*—makes a noose
cinch somewhere, rope reduced
to arousal, tightening. The pull,
the hard-learned feel of vertebrae supple
within a neck's column, and marrow's juice
sucked clean until what remains are flutes
of bone, a wind section of rubble.

Whenever I meet Mississippi in a dream,
it is always a landfill of labored breaths
or a grand mammal crippled in morass.
What did you ever want of us? I ask. It beams,
The same you want for me—the subtle heft
of razors beneath the magnolia tongue's lash.

CORMAC McCARTHY AS TRANSLATION

We are in Iowa City reading *The Road*
when Xiao Fan gently scolds us—

You Americans, always worried for,
always in need of saving, the world.

Were it not for the fact that I know
his sense of the American narrative

is steeped in bootleg Michael Bay
cinema from a Shanghai back-alley

contraband cave he'll drag me inside
months from now, I would consider

his critique. Maybe some of wisdom's
breath wafts within what he says.

Maybe he can see us clearly
—our bald-faced nationhood—

here against an unadorned middle
America, our god complex

so obvious when wreathed with lush
amber and green stalks. Another

misconception would that be,
for there is no such middle America.

Everywhere—or the need to be
everywhere—has no middle.

And, yes, planet America requires
saving. Maybe that is why our stories

all begin with the world almost ending
here. That keeps us up at night, shatters

our sleep—which Xiao Fan can't grasp
because he was never taught

our Pottery Barn rule: That if you've saved it,
then you've broken it. Then it's yours.

A HOUSE DIVIDED

On a railroad car in your America,
I made the acquaintance of a man
who sang a lifesong with these lyrics:
"Do whatever you can / to avoid
becoming a roofing man."
Maybe you would deem his tenor
elitist, or you would hear him as falling
off working-class key. He sang
not from his heart but his pulsing
imagination, where all roofs are
sloped like spires and Sequoia tall.
Who would wish for themselves or another
such a treacherous climb? In your America,
a clay-colored colt stomps, its hooves
cursing the barn's chronic lean.
In your America, blood pulses
within the fields, slow-poaching a mill saw's
buried flesh. In my America, my father
awakens again thankful that my face
is not the face returning his glare
from above eleven o'clock news
murder headlines. In his imagination,
the odds are just as convincing
that I would be posted on a corner
pushing powder instead of poems—
no reflection of him as a father nor me
as a son. We were merely born
in a city where the rues beyond our doors
were the *streets* that shanghaied souls.

To you, my America appears
distant, if even real at all, while you are
barely visible to me. Yet we continue
stealing glances at each other
from across the tattered hallways
of this overgrown house we call
a nation—a new wall erected
every minute, a bedroom added
beneath its leaking canopy of dreams.
We hear the dripping. We feel drafts
wrap cold fingers about our necks,
but neither you nor I trust each other
to hold the ladder or to ascend.

TWO YEARS FROM RETIREMENT,
MY NEIGHBOR CONTEMPLATES CANADA

We meet at our leaning wall of cinder
blocks that separate his yard from mine.
We've promised to right it plumb
every year. Up till now, all talk—no rebar,
no mortar. *$50 an hour*. Good money.
Damn good money, he seconds.
Arthritis now a hymn sung
by the choir of his cartilage, I measure
his gait's music as he climbs
four short notes back into his house
to retrieve the papers.
He brings back a dittoed leaflet
and a map of the northern territory
speckled with throbbing circles,
bull's-eyes. *Those are the job sites*—so many,
one must wonder what is Canada
building, or how it is that they lack
enough carpenters of their own.
My neighbor has faith that journey-
work in Canada will mean an escape
from the undocumented *Spanish boys*
and their nonunion, below-code labor,
which he blames for his paychecks
being unsteady, brittle these days.
I don't bother explaining globalism
to him—as if I understand it,
as if it threatens my livelihood
the same way it threatens his.
Good money—the lingua franca
in this age of quick growth, panoramic
decay. Our world becoming *old world*.

The new world just a flimsy Babel
tower. My neighbor must go build it
so he may one day drop his power drill
or bequeath it to me instead of his son,
who builds websites, his son, who will live
beyond us—a citizen of this shrinking
earth where no one will need to know
the leagues of salty blood, salty water
marking a Mexican from a Spaniard.
Our sleeping globe, it dreams this
one dream of expansion everlasting.

This jazz. Once you learn it as your own,
you will listen to the brassy chatter of backyard
mechanics as they riff on recent murders—

> *The boy who was killing folks*
> *One who had a claw hammer   No, in Virginia*
> *The boy slashing women's behinds*
> *No, sir, this boy was stabbing people, cold*

—seated on concave milk crates
or their sweat- and engine-
oil-anointed limbs drooping
off a pickup truck's gate, all slack
save for their fingers clutching cold beer.

Through appreciation, you will learn
to distinguish the hollers of youngins
that end in sweet jabs and dap
from the hollers that will summon
red and blue lights up the hill.

                    Electricity
drowns the nights. The restless
birds sing back to the evening
gunshots—the magnum's baritone *pow.*

With age, you'll come to fear June's music—
its melodies of bleeding boys, uneven
tempo of jacking, of strong-arm theft
omitted from newspapers. *They want
to get white folk moving
over here*. No transcribed tunes.
These notes puncture, lodge in vertebrae,
make jukeboxes of our spines.

This living—to be erect with song,
and then be bent by it.

JAGGED SERENADE

SONG OF THE WOMEN AND CHILDREN

Sing steady, woman, as you draw
the life jacket flush against your torso.

Sing before you thread survival
commands through the toddlers' ears:
Hold on to me. Do not let go.

At dry dock, the men carved this barge
from a solid slab of hubris. Now it sinks,

woman, and its sinking begs your presence
no more than its crafting called for.
Leave the men to what they call destiny.

For them, what will be nobler than dying
in the belly of their handmade whale?

Leave them thinking, "This devouring,
we invited upon ourselves"—they'll come
no closer to believing their hands are fate's.

There is no space for your resentment
in the life raft nor in your gut—that hold

just above your birthing grotto. Fill yourself
with the song—sing. Do not sink. You must
be buoyant. When rescue is slow to arrive,

you will need to drop anchor, give
the ocean your limbs. Swell, become

some small continent— terra firma where
the children's soles can rest. Damp. Shivering.
Let them hide in your scalp's forest. Lie. Sing

that their fathers were towed *home*—corpses pulled
over seas' sharp lips, swallowed by distant orange.

SUPREMATIST SWEET NOTHINGS

~after Malevich

My mouth is a hammer without
a handle or a handle
with an absent strike-head—a black bar
that could be a violin. My mouth's
ballad: *Every piece of you*
feels like a nail
against my lips. Sweet impact
—reverberation—draws me
again to the Rorschach of your form:
its archipelago today,
its crucifix yesterday,
its graffitied moth tomorrow.

Mirror, mirror—so many shapes
we become when we see not skin
but our own bald desires grafted
over each other's soft faces.
Speak your want. Speak my body
into a wind chime—a body
all clanging and imperceptible bones.
Then speak simply
for the sake of breath's nudging.
Make of me not song but singing.

O, BRIDE

~after Roy DeCarava's "Graduation 1949"

There is such a thing as local apocalypse.

You know this is true because I left you
there on the corner of *do you take*
and *till death*—standing in that dust lot.

How stark your dress in that caucus
of shadows. How stark the promise
upon which you forever gaze: a white-walled
Chevrolet on worn billboard, inside
a family—"white"—pasted in our dark land.

You should have known
that advertisement would never be us,
not in this nation of brown
ghettos urged to eat
themselves. Riots—not indigestion
but famishment sated with fire,
cracking glass, and blood.

The Black, the White—this country's beloved
abstractions. Sunlight, too, has made
two of you—one fabric, one shadow.

Fabric still waits for me. Shadow accepts
that I've been swallowed by the maw
of city blight. Shadow knows
the detritus and brick, knows it is now
wedded to an abandoned hand-drawn cart,
to a burden that must be gathered, like light,
and towed toward a dawn beyond the lens.

BEASTHEART

> I feel just like a stranger in the land where I was born.
> ~RICHIE HAVENS

You grope beneath the bed for the dated,
dusty phone book you last used
to kill a wolf spider. Your fingers flip
toward the Ds. You want "Dojo,"
but phone books lack such sophistication.
You regroup your digits, span
"Embroidery"   "Fire"   "Glaziers"
"Hypnotherapists"   "Insurance"   "Jewelers"
until you find a number under "Karate,"
which you dial. When a voice greets you,
you tell the voice, "I'd like to learn
how to hurt people." There is some edict
under which the voice cannot promise
to grant such requests, but it's a recession.
The voice says, "We're having a sale on pain,
actually—two for the price of one."
So many people you could invite to learn
the art of pain—to spar against—
and all that hurting would be condoned
inside the dojo. You can't resist a bargain
as morning sunlight against your skin summons
rage's larvae to poke through your pores,
and you begin morphing into that walking
abomination, the beastheart that despises
your "white" friends for the ease with which
they couple, the ease with which they offer,
"Try dating outside of your race" (ignorant
of all aside from color's tattered flags
and where those faux boundaries lie)

The beastheart feeds off your frustration,
your cyclical failure at finding love
with another who is brown like you, negro like
you, human like you. Has America made
you inhuman for wanting to love someone
like you, birth someone like you?
Downtown, the array of lovers urges you
to rebuke the beastheart, its lust
for pain. You could join the blissful
binary of pale hand / brown hand
interlocked. "Breed the next Obama"
or unremarkable mulatto. "Mixed people
are the most beautiful, don't you think?"
The beastheart doesn't think. It hungers
to find a dojo and kick the crap out of all comers
because inside you are "black" in America,
because you tempt the beastheart every time
you try and fail at loving another person
wrapped in "blackness." Knocked flat,
again. America towering over you
like Ali over Liston, like Love over Teddy P.
—crooning, "I think you'd better let it go."

CAPTURE MYOPATHY

Men are myths of composure. (They'll banish
a brother who won't disguise his fear.) How sage

the moustache, how proven the jaw

on a *real man*, no? Then let a woman arouse
amorous pinpricks within him. He'll muse,

"O, chère, you drive me to madness"—a ruse,

for *madness* is no destination, no land
separated from *masculine* by crimson bluffs,

nor is madness a pillaging horde

sent forth from women's various lips,
sent forth to scale those cliffs

and raze the houses of men—upending them

onto their chimneys. Beneath their veneers,
men are stampedes—not of once-bitten beasts

but of ones who run because the world is

running around them. A man cannot flee
a threat he does not understand

without revealing he does not understand.

It calls for a cloak of poise. If men could
slow down, listen to their thumping

little animal hearts, they might realize

there are worse fates in life than
being gobbled by a gorgeous predator.

I can't say it is the reason he called me,
but I'll remember it as the conversation
in which my friend divulged
that a mutual acquaintance gives
amazing head. He may have even said
brains or *dome*—his lingo rising farther
and farther away from the act.
My friends enlist me in these wars
of knowledge, priming my imagination
to conjure women I know only casually
with mouthfuls of phallus. Personally,
I don't enjoy head. That I cannot say
around other men. I'd feel more
comfortable walking toward the Pentagon
shouting *insha'Allah*. It's treasonous
for a man to admit he doesn't relish
fellatio. In my nightmares, other men
smash in my bedroom door, drag me
from sleep, accuse *you started this*
the day the world's women deny them
their fantasy's privilege. But I seek
no revolution—too messy. The truth is
there's no easier way to find a woman
who will offer you head than to confess
that you do not like it. *Well,*
you haven't had me do it. The matter
is not one of personal technique. Women
don't believe me when I say that as a boy
there was no retort that cut deeper
than to bark back at a boy *suck my dick*—
maybe a *bitch* added for punctuation.

I can't separate that history from the act,
can't think of head as casual, as a gesture
other than subjugation. Some women
claim they feel powerful taming the lower
serpent. I think, in the mind's recesses,
their men mouth *suck my dick, bitch*—
getting off on the penitent posture,
the bobbing bow. I cannot judge.
I simply want no part of the battle
between affection and dominance,
but even that is not true. I love
to enlist my tongue in name
of wracking—to pin down the pelvis
and fiddle over the clitoris as though
with each graze of my tongue
it becomes a new bead on an endless
rosary of release. *This isn't fair.*
You won't let me do that for you.
I'm accused of stubbornness, fear
of my own vulnerability. I say *it's my body*—
I have the right to refuse any touch
just as much as you have the right
to tell me stop. Do you want me to stop?—
to retreat, I ask disingenuously.
I ask without removing my lips.

NOSTALGIA

You promised to tell us, one student says
just before I dispatch them into the blind
freedom of semester's end. I pause.
Fine, but guess first. They pause.
A salvo of numbers then peppers my face,
too many. I listen for consensus—
twenty-eight! I pause, ponder.
I was twenty-eight three years ago.

If my face is still the face of who I was then,
I worry my students can read the map of me—
see the pushpin puncturing Yola's
paper soil. Nigeria was stealing
a woman from me. No. She chose
leaving, then longed afterward. My body
was a censer in which burned bits of Africa.
How I held my smoke, how it stained
my mouth, my nose. Everything
tasted of sacrilege—hating the continent
as I could not bring myself to hate her
while my limbs roamed the plains
of my bed—plain with her absence.

All the want is still there, rising
through my skin, lying to my students
about who it is that stands before them—
throat still smoked, sinuses clogged
in this season of pollen's release.

But there are times when I feel
my nose is just some weak felon
tied against my face, that if touched just so—
no bruising punch or slap but a gentle pinch—
ash would billow forth like confession.

NOTE BLUE

or POEM FOR EIGHTIES BABIES

(~also for T. P., 1950–2010)

If it's Teddy singing it—*don't leave me*
this way—it isn't the arrangement
your parents spun themselves through,
becoming another strobe-lit dervish. Listen
as it pounds. Think of them instead
not dancing but stilled in a corner,
buttressed by their own sweat
and clairvoyant uncertainty. Every plea,
every atonement that reaches sweet
and hard from Teddy's vocal folds,
is ambivalent toward their present,
its travails—the night humid, reduced to tissue
paper's fragility. It's June 1976, years before
code like *mother* and *father*—before either
is prepared to admit they could not imagine
the uphill slope of love after disco's
tongue licked the vinyl unfurrowed and the babies
—babies that began as mere pheromone
exchanges on a dance floor—
began falling into their young laps.
It isn't your fault. You did not stop the music.
Or if you did, it was Thelma Houston's cover,
not this bearded prayer of negative capability—
the *pleaseplease* under each pace your parents took
beyond the cusp of realizing nothing so good
could stay that good so long.

DIRGE IN APRIL

> Spend all your time writing love songs,
> but you don't love me.
> ~LIANNE LA HAVAS

As much as green is wilted white
the color of spring. And when
the public-radio street reporter describes
this morning sky's hue as *gun metal*,
I sense, immediately, that he has never
caressed a denuded gun—never judged
its skin against his own hide. This
mauve sky's threat is too soft a song
to coax a bullet from a barrel-throat.

Overcast atmosphere. I am fretting
spring's first rain, its larceny—the cherry
blossoms snatched by a cool cascade,
leaving any petals not swept down gutters
to spoil and crisp on my sidewalk.
Renewal's season always starts with this
extinguishing—before any tulip begins
stripping down to its stamen,
before hosta stems stab free
from the earth. First, this loss
of blossoms—a small heartbreak
followed by bit-lip humming
that somehow heals.

SONG OF THE MEN

There is an awful sound
in your skull—a din
you were not born with.
It is not the ambient noise
from your mother's womb,
though it is a sound that fills
your sinus, throat, and ear caverns
like an amniotic humor.
Maybe it comforts you, though
its reverb inflames your eyes,
troubles all that you see.
Some have dubbed the sound
patriarchy. Others name it
privilege—both broad
in frequency. What do you hear?
Have you the time to answer—
so busy raising and pounding
your mallet against the earth's
drumhead, constructing
new noises to drown out
that colonizing sound. In the absence
of a mallet or world to drum,
you become a dangerous being—
unable to make music to mask
that clamor you feel you cannot
silence. No work chant will save
you. Instead, turn the drum mallet
upon yourself—not to batter
but to dig down and excise
whatever within your head whirs
at this pitch that will kill you.

CONVERSATIONS WITH SLEEP

Violent lives ending violently. We never die in bed.

~RORSCHACH

CONVERSATIONS WITH SLEEP (I)

When rainwater swamped the lawn,
salamanders fled into the basement,
and when runoff breached
the cellar door, those slight
burgundy bodies groped blindly
for the crawlspace of my dreams.

This winter's vice has been too loose
to keep daffodils from sprouting through
the earth's skull. Tiny heads
themselves aching to bloom too soon
—more mouths. Winter still
a recession. Who will feed
more mouths?

                    I watched
with worry—hung my head outside—
then forgot to shut the window,
and now, Sleep, you've crawled in to do what?
What—lay an old lover's name on my chest
like some big cat offering a kill,
a winged name that should have migrated
beyond memory by now? Must I fold
its flightlessness into my dreaming too?
Must I fit my head between your wild jaws
as though it is you, Sleep, and not I
who has been trained to be gentle?

Sleep, I looked on while you had your way
with that woman on the metro. How noble—
her late shift hauling baggage at Reagan
left her so weak that you could drape her
body across both seats, her neck and head
cantilevered over the train's aisle.

Inevitably, when you pose us—our bones
not bones but wire—we go slack.
Your current in the wire quells our muscle,
our will. You odd sculptor, how you work us
from statues back into clay. Always,
you need to see us as earth. Patience—
we will return to dirt one day.

I know you did not make him, did not weave the flesh of this boy set adrift on his own subconscious and now run aground on my shoulder. I know his breath's apneic ebb and flow is not your doing, but tell me, Sleep, how did you make him mine, make me his evening dock? He does not know my name. No more than seatmates on a short flight, we ascend and his head sinks into my side with a trust so foreign to me. I am no pack animal. I am only at peace when bedded down within a huddle of my own limbs—no others—as I have always been. Have I not? Tell me, Sleep, have you ever made me rest my body against a stranger's? Speak. I will not accept the absence of restlessness in this child as an answer—this involuntary truss of his dreaming propped against my disbelief.

CONVERSATIONS WITH SLEEP (IV)

They don't lurch forth from the twiggy brush
of narrative—these wolves I dream of, Sleep.

I could be walking along a car-choked road
when, like wind-spun dust, they billow—
packs of fur and fangs. They swirl to life
and rampage around me. I flee.
Any and all in the vicinity run. Though
they are my dreams, the wolves
chase who they choose—mauling
the pedestrians of my mind.

Every door in sight a glass door. Wolf eyes
turn toward me, and I duck into a storefront
or office just before they pounce
—wet noses and snapping jaws mashed
against glass, a specimen of hunger.

Have you read the Dream Book, Sleep?
(Maybe you wrote it?) It claims my middle
brain either hungers or feels hunted.
But our dreams are the anterooms
between quickness and death—where
we divest of meaning's demands.

So, say I dream
of wolves for their appetites draw them
to my subconscious's gray habitat, and there
they feed before taking their mouths,
bejeweled with blood, to stalk another's.

Each night that we've survived you,
Sleep, we've spared ourselves
a death. In bed, the restive mind
is a power line snapped in a storm
of earthly ruckus. It thwacks
black pavement, wails hot orange
confetti—all of it an aching
plea to rejoin the continuum,
plug back into the violent world.
Our faces reply with twitching eyes
that jostle beneath thin eyelids
until those shutters part and we squint
our way into a new day.

        We do not beg the night
for placid slumber. One evening,
rest will come for us—that release
deemed *heavenly*, called *peace*.
But in your grip, Sleep, may our thoughts
riot against rest. May our minds fret
they are under siege by a relentless
world, for that is what riles us
up from indifferent bedsprings—
sweaty, palpitating, awake.

ESCHATOLOGY

IT IS ALWAYS DARK IN EGYPT

by the time tripods erect themselves
and foreign reporters have schlepped
back to their high hotels following sorties
into Tahrir Square. They proffer news
on a platter of night—the camera
scouring the black-green vistas,
then spotting a Molotov tumbling
end over end through the air
until it bursts on the back of a man
fleeing, blooming into wings of flame.
We know burning pinions do not soar
but, rather, embrace the body
until its writhing is no more.

Anglophone anchors pose questions
the dark won't translate: *Are these
protestors or Mubarak supporters
being set aflame, being dragged
into a hollow of fists and kicks?*
From this transatlantic vantage,
a bleeding stalemate is all we can see,
and all I know for certain is that
I haven't spoken with my father
for the past two months—since before
Tunisia even. I can't remember
a reason. Something about a snowstorm
or about leaving my cell phone set
to silent too often—all his calls
I never seem to receive. A voice message,
my father barking in his language of goddamns.

I want to believe both my silence and this protest
are peaceful, but bodies are sprawled
still on Cairo's streets, chants beginning
to sharpen the spade for Mubarak's grave.
This is the point at which good is susceptible
to chaos's seduction—when a former general's
stubbornness blossoms larger than a nation's
rebuke or where my pride grows heavier
than the nudge for a father and son to speak.

A week from now, he'll give in—
ceding to the Egyptians' coalition.
Amid so many exhales, a man will kiss
a bottle to then push the liquid, his lungs,
through a flambeau's head—the fireball
a landing beacon for the new day: *here.*
And I will be wishing that a winter
storm had not become an ice wall between
my father and I—wishing that we
could be watching the world change
together, a thaw. I never called.

BARCODE

~after "Numberology, AP" by Claudia Vess

Morning does not begin until
the sun's pupil scans my face,
reads the microscopic numbers
marked by the thin bars
of my pursed eyelids or lips.

Each day, my history is becoming
data, yours too. Even the years'
digits have been assigned
digits. I was born in the year
of the monkey, with an infant
hernia whose ghost pain
still shrieks when I ride
in a car or plane or coaster
that plummets sharply
(info encrypted in the lines
of my eyebrow, etched in thin
integers on hairs' spines).

How daylight distinguishes us
now, how the moon knows when
our blood has expired—time
to erase our faces, save our data
in the flesh of another,
and order the earth restore
our bodies to uncoded pulp.

This system: such efficiency. Soon
none of us will need our given names.

with clear-cased woofers for heads,
no eyes. They see us as a bat sees
a mosquito—a fleshy echo,
a morsel of sound. You've heard
their intergalactic tour busses
purring at our stratosphere's curb.
They await counterintelligence
transmissions from our laptops
and our blue teeth, await word
of humanity's critical mass,
our ripening. How many times
have we dreamed it this way:
the Age of the Machines,
postindustrial terrors whose
tempered paws—five welded fingers
—wrench back our roofs,
siderophilic tongues seeking blood,
licking the crumbs of us from our beds.
O, great nation, it won't be pretty.
What land will we now barter
for our lives? A treaty inked
in advance of the metal ones' footfall.
Give them Gary. Give them Detroit,
Pittsburgh, Braddock—those forgotten
nurseries of girders and axels.
Tell the machines we honor their dead,
distant cousins. Tell them
we tendered those cities to repose

out of respect for welded steel's
bygone era. Tell them Ford
and Carnegie were giant men, that war
glazed their palms with gold.
Tell them we soft beings mourn
manufacture's death as our own.

FOOL'S THERAPY

~for Rob and other dead "Bees"

Robert Peace is dead. Those words, writing them,
should assuage something. They do not—
they say nothing of his gruff brilliance, nor lure
my mind to parse the syntax of his passing.

I still envy the ease with which Peace untangled
derivatives—he helped me feel the relief
of not being the smartest head in the classroom
(a grace that serves any fool well in later life).

Still, Peace could also say the droll things
that needed saying, as he did during religion class
—his eyes absent, off reading through the window
what awaited us beyond senior year, beyond Newark.

He opined, "Beyoncé is so fine, I'd drink her bathwater."
His hyperbole turned my stomach—recalling too well
what I'd learned of the body and what it secretes,
knowing too little of lust. What was it then

Peace was teaching me? My mind too busy
mulling what Father Matthew meant by saying,
"Sex without love is no more than masturbation."
(He meant if you seek pleasure, seek pleasure,

not acts of love.) I inflate my basketball
the day after I learn Peace has been shot, has died.
I walk onto a giving plane of hardwood
and flick three-pointers at the hoop—not in love

with the world, just wanting it to grant me
simple pleasure, the release of releasing
the ball from my fingertips. No teenager,
my knees now burn with each leap and drift,

but at least I can predict what follows here.
Peace is dead. I please myself with shooting jumpers.
Sneaker-squeak, tap of landing, swish of contact—
the sequence a sonic salve. I don't love the world

in this moment. I do as Father Matthew taught us.

GOLIATH

... And there it rises before us—
growing against our own disbelief
that god would grant a mountain legs
and arms and fists. For we phalanx
men, all our resolve wells from muscle
memory, not understanding.
We only understand how to aim
our pikes, tense our taxed torsos.
We are the grunts this world needs
to perish first. A lesson of blood
the goliath teaches us—
how the slurry of our defeated flesh
and bones will lube the clicking
gears in the earth's clock core.
For we small men—not of stature
but of worth to the human
machine—for us seconds are
a deficient measure of time.
More exact are the pounding feet
of fate, that somber opening
rhythm in each of the goliath's dances,
be it battle's foxtrot or the sweeping
waltzes of plague or recession.
We are the ones who suffer first
so men of prestige, men of means,
are spared—so their folly may again rouse
the goliath, slayer of common men.

EXIT SEASON

~for 2012, a voracious year

An oak splintered by winter
wind reveals the riddled marrow
termites have made of its heartwood—
a rusted core echoing rusted leaves.

Once, a not-quite-old man told me
he admired winter for its cold
hands, how they tuck the elderly
into their final sleep.

This season's visual confusion—
rivers swelled to a plush brown,
grasses frost-baked to ash.

Born in November's anticipation,
each year, I can only long for spring's
ripening through the frigid months'
dusky whispers. I play deaf as the season
tries its hand at charades. *One word*,
it pantomimes. *Survive*, I answer
before snow can remember to fall.

WORDS FOR THE DEPARTED

~for the Batipps family, 06.09.2012

These words, difficult to see.
Their letters hang, sway like paper
lanterns unlit in a fog—faint
outlines, not one shape clear
enough for our eyes to trace
or transmit back to the brain's
den of interpretation.
For these reasons, we often cannot
speak the words we yearn to give
the people who have left us
for that shrouded spirit realm
that is mute with our ignorance
of what comes after the last steps
we tread on earth. We are born
to leave this place. We are born
to eventually enter another.
Two realms—and to be human
and still breathing
is to be blind to that angelpath
ahead of us. Still there exists
a third realm—not of bodies or souls
but the miscellany of life sketched
along the interiors of our skulls.
It is primitive and imprecise.
It is memory—our pilot light,
which may not spark each lantern letter
but will make enough flames bloom
so that we may spell the names

of those who have departed,
so that we may breathe
remembrance into this fog of absence,
parting it—not calling our lost back but
proving they once stood among us.

CHARM

Stowed just behind my ear,
hidden yet within quick recall:

this memory of the Mamdouhi sisters
and the dance they danced
before a capacity audience of me.

I had crossed the Lambeth common,
climbed the stairs to the younger's
dorm room—in need of some book
whose importance withered once
I arrived and they asked if I wanted
to see them move together.

Too shy to say "yes" with confidence.
Too *man* to not say "sure." (Today,
I would say "please." I would
say "thank you" before such a gift
is given.) Precision. Synchronized
sisters. Transfixed—such a stiff word.
Give me a term that blends
guilt and awe, makes a duet
of those feelings. It would name
that swirl in my gut as I trained
my gaze to their sharpened feet, pursed
thumbs and index fingers, blinking
eyes like chimes. I wondered
who was I to be offered their dance
homework. Who would believe
what I was being shown? I studied,
made an art of being present, certain
this recital would never happen again.

___

As I later floated from their room,
my father's voice shook my skull:
Son, life is all downhill after college.
I stash the memory of their dance
for the days when I feel my father
just might be right, and I'm descending
midlife's gyre. I've been lucky—I saw
some of the summit. I can remember
that I'm tumbling from an apex of grace.

THE MEDIOCRITY PRINCIPLE

I am watching the stars, admiring their complex trajectories
through space, through time. I am trying to give a name to
the force that set them in motion.

~DR. MANHATTAN

CONTEXT

I know this about my body—it has edges.

Its surface swelled against, chafed,

my mother's viscera and was seasoned there.

This truth a truth that fits within another.

You tell me the truth of our universe

begins with a big bang. I say that bang

was simply a body. Thus, there must be a body,

a form, from which the rough energy

and atoms rocketed free. Bang. I cried

when the white coat pulled my slick head

free from my mother. I never made a sound

while within her, but I was there—a pulsing

potential, a fly in a fist, bound but not

crushed. What applied the pressure

necessary to mash egg and seed or dark

matter and fire toward the tipping point

of birth? I'll accept your theory, your big bang,

but what body first housed those elements?

There are no sourceless starts.

My body tells me a presence preceded, a body

that compressed, propelled what would become

the universe—the ever-echoing wail.

POINTS OF CONTACT

Name one revolution whose inception was unlike a fist.
Factions disparate, then tucked together—coiled like a fist.

Foreign policies are symbol languages—idiomatic, cryptic.
In America, nothing says "We desire peace" like a fist.

The heart is a one-man rave in the body's industrial district.
Blooddrunk and insomniac, it pumps toward sleep like a fist.

Mammogram magic revealed my lover's dense breasts.
Behind each nipple I kissed, a soft knot threatened her like a fist.

Our universe's yet shattered mysteries fear the astrophysicist.
"Damn his galaxies-thick glasses, his mind, relentless, like a fist."

"Like a glove"—the young groom exalts his wife's love, its fit.
Sounds romantic. (He means sex—her *love's* grip like a fist.)

"An unfocused punch, Kyle, risks a broken hand or wrist."
So laden the psyches of men. Father, must I also think like a fist?

CALL AND RESPONSE

~A mash-up of the Lord's Prayer and "The Message"

Our Father who art in heaven,
there's broken glass everywhere.
Thy hallowed staircase pissed on
by those who care not
for thy kingdom, thy name.
Come—thy will be the smell.
Thy will be the noise
on Earth. In heaven, no
money moves. Give us
this day our rats in the front room,
our roaches in the back,
and forgive the junkie
in the alley, his baseball bat.
But trespass in this place
we try to get away from. Repossess
those who've trespassed against us.
Lead us, but do not push—
we're so close to the edge of temptation.
Deliver us from our lost
heads—this evil trying us.
For thine kingdom is like a jungle.
Sometimes, it makes us wonder
how your power keeps.
We go under. Glory
forever?—a ha-ha ha ha.
Amen.

EUCHARIST

God the locksmith. God
the language. The unfinished
suits of us. God the tailor.
God the light-
house and tempest. God
the immune system. Afflicted,
we. God the earthen
path. God the cross-vaulted
and high. God the un-everything—
as in the alpha inscribed
between the omega's labia.
God the I. God the histamine
inhibitor. Bless me.
May our heads split to see
the gods within our God.
God the stained-
glass window: spectrum
of unraveled white
light. God the father
of the bait (hook, line,
sink into us)—the word
of prophets and a son
who dissolves on our tongues.

REVERENCE IN THE ATOMIC AGE

Pair me—lay me
covalent—with a breathing
body that would not laugh
were I to proclaim, *Salvador*
Dalí was god
come to frolic upon earth,

a body who would allow
my fingers to scribble inert
scriptures across her forehead
as Dali brushed Medusa's visage
over Gala's blank brow.

Looking into his wife's eyes
turned Salvador soft, not stone,
turned him to flammable.
I want that—this world
already full of statues.
My mouth is a plinth
piled with plutonium
isotopes waiting
to be split with a kiss.

DEAR RELIGION

Listen now to something human.

~LI-YOUNG LEE

First is urge, then the urge to act
upon urge—the former absolute
impulse, so cellular, buried
so far within us that to grope for it
would require we delve
down beyond flesh, threaten
to breach that brisk unknown
for which our bodies serve as dams.

What if it is resonance and not sin
that is original? Each heart pulse,
each lung swell: *urge, urge,*
urge. Steady and metronomic—
desire's tempo. Urge: the faint
tapping that knows the body
longs to slow drag, to prance,
boogie.

       The righteous choir
chides "all the earth's surfaces
are not dance floors." Fine,
but cannot we know restraint
without muting the bottom,
corporeal beat: *urge, urge, urge.*
Our ears must chew the cud of it—
mastication marking us
not cloven but blessedly human.

MAN ON AN IRON SHORE

"What train is this?" asks an adolescent
with burnt peach curls, with cutoffs quite
short for the few years her face holds,
thighs too slim to distend the denim.
She wants New York. She wants you
to assure her that this train won't stop
at Secaucus—that the line will continue
coring rock and darkness until arrival,
slow and dirty, in the city that awaits
no one, the city whose eyes
crack groggily only to peer above
thousands of feet unclean—multiplying
and pressing down avenues
in search of whatever they believe
the city's name has promised.

You are not the city. You are a man,
though not a father nor brother by blood.
You could tell the girl, "Wrong train"—
her desired destination is a den
not for adolescents racing against
their girlhood. Feel your own age, recall
a time when you would have longed
to serve as her Charon—young
and bored with ferrying yet willing
to promise her soul's safe passage
in exchange for a phone number
scribbled into the meat of your palm.

That boy is no longer you. Tonight,
want only to befuddle her, to leave her
wandering Newark Penn's platforms
until frustration ushers her home pouting
as you want (no, need) to remember her
now that you are a man who has ruined
and has seen ruin.

But one lie will not damn her flood—your noble
deceit no more than a hitch in her evening.
Know she will ask another. Just tell her,
"New York," and forget the word "girl"—silence
whatever chaste bell it rings in your mind.
Drown it in the chime of closing doors.

> God blessed them and said to them, "Be fruitful and
> increase in number; fill the earth and subdue it."
> ~GENESIS 1:28 (NIV)

I walked among men for a year
with the task of pausing if I heard
one speak the words, "I fucked her."
At that point, I'd produce for them
a sketch pad and kindly request
drawings of what each man implied.

Those too shy only stared
at uninked pages. *No shame*,
I assured. *God knows what you google—*
those "Os" his eyes—and still
you have not been struck down.
So draw. Some began tracing
from memories the curves and buds
of breasts. *No, give me symbols.*
Give me act, I implored. They drew
boulders crushing other boulders
into sand or guns fired point-blank
through panes of ice. One drew
a pickup truck—its revving tires
stripping pelts from the dirt road.
The trend was one of leaving
something marred if not wholly
shattered.

I was not bold enough
to ask those men-turned-artists
if they'd desire what they drew, to be
themselves *fucked*. Rather, I inquired why
they thought the women wanted
what their art promised. One: "It's not
women. It's their bodies. The earth
breaks, desires to be broken."
Another: "The girls— I mean, they beg
'harder, harder.' They say it—'Fuck me'"—
deaf to the ways language acts as landscape.

What if the women are only speaking back
to the easels they see behind male eyes?
Imagine if god had appeared before man
as the self-portrait of a woman. Would they
have listened when she did not sketch
the earth as a body men needed to subdue?

MULLIGAN

If I've failed as a man, upon expiring
I'll be returned to this fuzzy rock
as a koi. I'll swell against enclosure
like an American (again), but
this time it will be my body
bloating instead of my ego.

I pray I do not fail. I lament
the life of bright fish in ponds—
mouths cleaving water, gasping
with no language to expel.

That is why we love dolphins.
They're what we dream of—talking fish,
what we hope fortune's wheel will stop on
should the gods dial back our evolution.

But I'm certain that if I fail,
I'll be brought back as a silent, ornamental
koi and not a dolphin. I've already said
enough in this life—me and my big, wet mouth.

NONE OF US SAINTS

~for Ruth Dargan

Tell me who presides over the service
when the minister's mother has died.
Whose hands attempt to lift him? Who
surveys his self-anointing face, explains,
This is the Lord's will—the cancer
that swam through and seized the body
in which the preacher's flesh first firmed?

Thou art a rock. Thou hast shown thyself
firm. Maybe. It's possible he could
right himself—weak though giving
his weight to the pulpit—and raise
his mother's spirit skyward with the wind
aid of God's breath. But, no,
he would be more human than holy
at her passing—more Adam than angel.

Let him remain on the floor—
saliva and tears blended on his lips as he begs,
No talk of God—my mother is dead.

Tell me where I'll find that preacher.
He is the one I will summon
to send my dying grandmother *home*—
a man, not a rock—for none here are Peter,
none of us saints. We are braids
tied between birth and death's buoys.
None of us know that dark
sea beneath, but bring me the preacher
who can cry, who I can see
brims with salt and water.

UNLESS MAROONED

never pen a message and set it adrift
in a bottle you have not drained
with your own lips. Your words

need to be heavy with what once
sloshed within that glass—be it port

or a malbec's harsh blood.
The tongue should be coated—
not only the enunciating knot

of muscle in the mouth's locket,
but, too, that subvocal tongue

that hums with each word heard
in your mind as you write.
A bottle's chance of arrival will rise

if you fill the cavity beneath the cork
with more than ink, paper, and air.

So first swallow. Break down
sugars and tannins—you are
a refinery. With the grape's blood

now in your blood, write "I have
drunk. I am lost. Come find me."

PALE BLUE DOT

We're far enough from heaven. Now, we can freak out.

~DEEP COTTON

Either a romantic or subtle sadist,
Carl Sagan begged NASA to burn
Voyager's hydrazine thrusters,
rotating her hull so she might
capture one last snapshot
before drifting beyond radio
tether—exiting the literal
edge of our galaxy.
The image she spat back:
bands of deconstructed rainbow
and one blue speck. *That's us,*
some astronomer gasped
once the matter of his mind
could discern our infinitesimal
everything wrapped in blue
fabric—atmosphere's loomed light,
which we recognize from pristine
days when our eyes pan upward.
Though we have that photograph,
only Voyager has felt the cold
pull of witnessing all that we are
fitted on the head of a pin
pushed into a black expanse
wider than any sky we'll ever face.

NOTES

Opening: Epigraph taken from "Sooner or Later" on N.E.R.D's album *Seeing Sounds* (Star Trak, 2008).

"Within the Break: An Author's Note": Epigraph taken from Fred Joiner's poem "Song for Anacostia" published in *Full Moon on K Street: Poems About Washington, D.C.* (Alexandria, Va.: Plan B, 2009).

"China Syndrome or Slow Ride from Logan to the Heights": The WMATA 54 bus line, running up Fourteenth Street, connects the Logan Circle and Columbia Heights neighborhoods in northwest Washington, D.C.

"O, Ghost": Title comes from the closing of Terrance Hayes's poem "Shakur" published in the collection *Lighthead* (New York: Penguin, 2010).

"States May Sing Their Songs of Praise": Title comes from the first line of the Mississippi state song.

"We / Die Soon": Title comes from the closing of Gwendolyn Brooks's poem "We Real Cool" published in *The Bean Easters* (New York: Harpers, 1960).

"Beastheart": Epigraph taken from "What About Me," the lead track on Richie Havens's album *The Great Blind Degree* (Stormy Forest, 1971).

"Dirge in April": Epigraph taken from the song "Forget" on Lianne La Havas's album *Is Your Love Big Enough?* (Warner Bros., 2012).

Conversations with Sleep: Epigraph taken from the character Rorschach as spoken in *Watchmen*, no. 2, written by Alan Moore and originally published by DC Comics, October 1986.

The Mediocrity Principle: Epigraph taken from the character Dr. Manhattan as spoken in *Watchmen*, no. 4, written by Alan Moore and originally published by DC Comics, December 1986.

"Dear Religion": Epigraph taken from Li-Young Lee's poem "Always a Rose," published in the collection *Rose* (Rochester, N.Y.: BOA Editions, 1993).

"Pale Blue Dot": Epigraph taken from "We're Far Enough from Heaven" on Deep Cotton's 2013 fixtape *Runaway Radio* (Wondaland, 2013).